The Pride of the Panthers

- Jeff Trippe

Silent E Publishing Company

Artwork & Cover by: E.P. Pirt
Copyright © 2014

First Print Edition
(Original Story first published electronically in 1999)

Silent E Publishing Company
4446 Hendricks Ave, #141
Jacksonville, Florida, USA
All Rights Reserved

ISBN-13 978-1-941091-00-5

10 9 8 7 6 5 4 3 2 1

For Philip

Table of Contents

Chapter One
A Generous Offer

There was never a time, so far as I remember, when I didn't play ice hockey in Port Royal, Maine. Likewise, I don't remember a time when my dad was not my coach. And that's why, the first time I got on the bus to New Hampshire, after putting my bags and sticks in the carrier underneath, I felt a little scared. But I was excited, too, and so ever since then, whenever I smell diesel fumes from a bus, I have the same feeling. It's the smell of the unknown, and it can be good or bad, but in a way you make it whatever it is.

On our way to the station that morning - a dark and early morning in the early fall with the chestnuts clattering on the hood of our old Bel-Air - Dad and I talked about the usual things, ordinary things, the way we always did on our way to hockey games. We talked about anything except hockey - about vacations we had taken as a family, about fishing maybe, or he would discuss an article he had read about stereos (that was his other favorite thing, aside from ice hockey). Of course, we knew it was different this time. I was going away to a school in another state, another town, to live in a dormitory with other boys and to play hockey on the school's team, and it would be weeks before I'd see my parents again or my little sister Rose. To tell the truth, even though I was almost thirteen years old, I didn't want to leave Port Royal.

Our town is small enough that if you were to go there, people would probably stare at you as you walked down the street. It's not because we're rude - it's just that everyone knows everyone else. Dad always says that this is both a curse and a blessing, and I suppose now that I have been away from home, I know what he means. It's comforting to see the same faces and to know what people will say and do, and who they will most likely vote for in the mayor's race, for instance, but new towns with new people help you understand that the world is a big place. There are lots of different ways to live.

Still, I missed the beginning of winter in Port Royal, when the last few leaves tear off and fly from the trees in our yard and spin away beyond our fence, and the sky changes colors, and then one morning on the walk to school you find that Fisher's Pond has frozen and it's time to play hockey

8

again. It's hard to describe playing hockey on a pond if you haven't done it. I've always played in youth leagues, on indoor rinks, and that's fine, but it's not the same feeling as skating on a pond at twilight with maybe one streetlamp to throw your shadow on the ice and the puck coming at you like a blurry black bullet. After a while you learn to sort of guess where the puck is or how fast it's coming. Mom said we would ruin our eyes, but Dad said it helped us to hone our hockey instincts, and maybe they were both right, because when I was nine I started wearing glasses for nearsightedness, but people still say I am one of the best players to come out of Port Royal since Pat Snee, who played in the American Hockey League in 1980. That's what they say, anyway.

I suppose I should tell how I happened to leave my hometown. Our bantam team, the Chiefs, was playing in a spring tournament last year in Portland, and a fellow in a checkered suit approached my dad after the game as we were packing up our station wagon for the trip back. His name was Mr. Withers, and he said he had a vacation home nearby and had just come out to the game for fun (he had no children of his own, he said) but was impressed by my game and wanted to come to Port Royal in a couple of weeks to talk to us about the possibility of my playing hockey for the Price School, a boys' boarding school in Concord, where he had used to be a coach but was now a sort of counselor. I recall that I did have a pretty good tournament, scoring four goals, I think, in two games. Anyway, my dad said it would be okay, although, as he told me much later, he never believed Mr. Withers would actually show up at our house. He did, though, and we all sat in the den, where my dad kept his old cabinet stereo and his jazz records (my dad will probably be one of the last people on earth still listening to long-playing albums), and Mr. Withers told us all about the Price School. He was fond of saying things such as "Wonderful place for a boy such as Gil," and "Perhaps it's time to think of Gil's future," but all in all he was a nice man and seemed very genuinely interested in me.

My mother sat completely rigid the whole time with her eyes narrowed, and I could tell she was against the idea, until Mr. Withers began talking about the school's academic record.

"Price's seniors have the highest median test scores in this part of the country," he said. "Our valedictorian last year is now attending Harvard." And so on. My mother's face softened slowly.

But there was the issue of money, my father said. He could never afford to send me to a school like Price. Mr. Withers had an answer for that, too.

"Don't let the money worry you just now. We have a financial plan set up for boys like Gil. Of course, he would have to pass our entrance exam. But it's such an opportunity for him, really. I'd hate to see him miss out on it."

I figured Mr. Withers must have been one heck of a counselor, because he managed to convince my parents that afternoon, and they are two of the hardest cases I've ever seen. Anyway, I took their entrance exam, and they notified us by mail in the spring. I would be going to the Price School for Boys the next fall.

I remember that at school the following day, I ran into two of my best friends, Hal Yates and Freddie Dixon. I had played hockey and baseball with them since we were five years old. Hal was big, with a flat-top haircut and freckles. Freddie was tall and thin, but was probably the best pitcher in town. I told them about the letter, and that I would be leaving Port Royal in a few months.

For a moment, neither of them said a word, as we headed for class. Then Hal stopped and stuck out his hand. "That's great news, Gil," he said. "I'm sure you'll do real well at Price." Freddie nodded in agreement.

"They've got a great reputation," he offered.

But I could tell that in that moment, something changed. That's how it is when you leave a place, I've learned. I didn't see the guys much that summer, but busied myself cutting lawns and swimming at the YMCA, trying to stay in shape.

And then one morning in early September, I found myself at the bus station. My dad had to go to work and couldn't drive me all that way, and besides, we all agreed, it would be a good experience to ride the bus on my own. Mr. Withers would meet me at the station in Concord. I might as well get used to being a little more independent. But if I had known how much my life was about to change, I doubt whether I would ever have said goodbye to my dad and gotten on that bus at all. As the gears crunched and we dieseled away, I looked back and watched as the treetops, some of which were just beginning to show hints of gold, swallowed up the last couple of church steeples, and for the first time, I think, I realized how small Port Royal really is. And just for a moment, I had the crazy idea that I might never see the place again.

Chapter Two

In A Strange Place

Boy, was I glad to see Mr. Withers. By the time we got to the station in Concord more than three hours later, I had eaten the peanut butter and banana sandwiches my father had made for me, and I was already feeling homesick. I guess it was because he had made the same kind of sandwiches so many times - when I left for boys camp in Canada, whenever we had a hockey tournament out of town, and nearly every day for school - and I felt a little empty myself when I looked at the crumbs in the empty sandwich bag. But Mr. Withers, who was wearing the same checkered coat as the last time I had seen him, was grinning at me like he was my old, long-lost uncle.

"Gil!" He patted my shoulders heartily.

"Hello, sir."

"How was your trip, son?"

"Oh, fine. I've been to New Hampshire before. Well, once anyway."

"Of course you have. Coach Nelson would have come for you himself, but he had some business back at school."

A tall, tussle-haired boy suddenly appeared at Mr. Withers' side. "Sir?" he said. "Let's not forget about that parking meter." He was a lean, wide-shouldered boy in khaki pants and a blue jacket with a big letter 'P' stitched in red. He looked coolly at me after he spoke, and there was something familiar to me in his bright green eyes.

"Right you are, Rocky," Mr. Withers said. "Oh, by the way. Gil Gibbs, this is Rocky Lufrano. You two will be teammates this season at Price. Rocky led the middle-school team in scoring last year, Gil."

I wasn't sure what to say... I felt certain I had seen this kid someplace before. Finally I stammered, "Hey... that's great... Good to meet you," but Rocky didn't meet my gaze. He was still looking at Mr. Withers, who was now busy dragging my bags from the compartment beneath the bus. I was used to carrying my own stuff and felt a bit strange walking along with my hands dangling as Mr. Withers manhandled my hockey bag and suitcase. Rocky had my two sticks, having slung them in their carrier over his shoulder. It was not a long ride from the station to the Price School. I had seen pictures of the place, but that didn't prepare me for the grandness of it all, the old brown-brick buildings, the bell tower, the green playing fields, and the tall, white birch trees which grew in an orderly row along the driveway. It was sort of like driving right into a postcard. There were a few boys going here and there in their blue Price jackets, balancing the stacks of books they would need for the new school year - they all knew where they were going and they all seemed to belong, and I will admit I felt anxious about it all. It seemed a million miles away from Port Royal. Mr. Withers must have read my thoughts, because he said,

"Now, Gil, don't worry about a thing. It looks a bit overwhelming, I know, but you'll be used to everything in no time. Rocky, can I trust you to take Gil up to his room and help him get situated?"

"Sure, Mr. Withers."

Still, I didn't feel much better. I missed my mom and dad and my little sister Rose. I missed my room at home, too, and that feeling was only made worse when I saw my new quarters: it was a very small dormitory room painted a pale green, and it smelled of ammonia and spray-on deodorant and somebody's unwashed laundry, with two narrow bunks attached to opposite walls. One half of the room was completely bare, with no sheets on the bunk and nothing on the walls. That was to be my side, I assumed, because the other side was crowded with some kid's junk - a desktop computer, some tangled-up clothes, a ragged pair of hockey skates, some music posters, and a couple of sticks leaned in the corner.

Rocky spoke to me directly for the first time: "You'll be rooming with Bailey. They try to keep all the players on the same floor. Oh, yeah, I almost forgot - we've got our first team meeting and practice today. Be down at the rink in your gear at two-thirty."

He was gone before I could even ask him where the rink was. And I had to go down and get my schoolbooks and supplies, and I wasn't sure how that worked either.

I looked around the dismal little room again. I thought about my bedroom at home, with the window overlooking our backyard, from which I could also see my neighbor's yard and treehouse. I liked to open it in the fall and let in the smell of wood-fires and burning leaves, and in the mornings this mingled with the smell of breakfast coming from downstairs - ham and eggs usually. Now I looked out of my new window, and it wasn't such a bad view - nice, really, with the broad green lawn leading straight to the stately bell tower. In fact, the bells were ringing at that instant, two o'clock. I tried to open the little window, but it was stuck fast.

I turned my attention to putting some of my things away. When I opened the closet, I saw the first sign that I had been expected or even had a place here. A navy-blue Price School blazer was hanging there, with the red and black striped tie draped around the hanger. It wasn't new, I guessed, but it was all right - a bit tight under the armpits when I tried it on, but at least now I would look more like I fit in. I ran my fingers over the fancy red stitching on the left breast pocket.

Just then the door opened and two boys came in noisily. They didn't notice me at first, as one of them flung an armload of heavy books onto the bunk and then struggled out of his coat and yanked at his tie. "Geez, I'm suffocating!" he said. Then he turned around and saw me. He was a short kid, really, but with a strong build and blond hair cut close to his scalp, and he grinned at me.

"Hey, it's the new kid," he said. "How ya' doin'?? I'm your roommate, name's Tom Bailey. Guys on the team call me Crunch."

At this, the other boy laughed. "Don't let him kid you," he said. "We call him Bailey. He wants us to call him Crunch, but he's more used to being crunched. My name is Clark Hightower." Each of them shook my hand in turn.

"I'm Gil Gibbs," I said.

Tom nodded. "We heard you were coming. So you're the new defenseman, eh?"

"I - I don't know," I stammered. "Usually I play center."

"That's what my last roommate said, too. He's no longer with us, as you can see."

"What do you mean?" I asked.

Clark Hightower spoke up: "He just means that Rocky has a lock on that position, is all, at least on the first line. It's not a good idea to challenge Rocky."

"What happened? Did he - your old roommate, I mean - did he get cut from the team?"

The two boys looked at one another. "Well, not exactly," Clark said.

"If you really want to know, he went back home to recover," Bailey said, "but he never actually made it back to school."

"Recover?"

"Yeah. Three cracked ribs and a broken wrist. It happened in practice last spring. Somebody checked him, see."

"Wow," I said. "Who would do that to his own teammate?"

Hightower and Bailey answered in unison: "Rocky."

My stunned surprise over this information must have been obvious. Tom grinned and poked me in the shoulder. "Hey, don't worry about it. Listen, roomie, you'd best go and collect your books and junk, if you're going to be on time for our first practice."

"Right," I said, and I busied myself putting away the rest of my things. Then I ventured out onto the campus to try and locate the bookstore. But all I could think of was Rocky Lufrano. What kind of kid would do something like that? Why did he seem to be so friendly with Mr. Withers? And I wondered whether they would really make me into a defenseman; that was fine with me if they did, but I didn't know whether I could be any good at defense.

21

Then, before I knew it, the bell tower was ringing: three o'clock. It was time to get ready for my first time on the ice as a member of the Price School Panthers.

Chapter Three
A Hard Shot

As it happened, I was almost late. I had some trouble finding my way around, first to the bookstore and then the ice arena. Then, of course, I dropped all my books - which must have weighed thirty pounds - in the stairwell. I dropped my laptop computer, too (the first one I'd ever had just for myself), but luckily it was in the thickly padded case. When I finally got to my room and flung everything onto the bunk, I realized that Tom Bailey had already dressed and gone; in fact, the whole hall was dead quiet.

Next, I couldn't find my elbow pads. At last I found them stuffed into the corner of the bag, and I grabbed my skates and sticks and rushed out of the dorm and across the quad. I saw a kid walking across the grass and breathlessly asked him which of the big buildings before me was the hockey rink.

"The gym and auditorium are to your left. Arena doors are on the right."

"Thanks."

I practically flew through the double doors and down the steps to the locker room. I didn't really have time to take it all in, but I did notice some big trophy cases in the lobby, and some old black and white photos of past teams, and I told myself I would have to take a closer look after practice. When I entered the locker room, Tom Bailey and Clark Hightower were just on their way out the door that led to the ramp and the ice.

"Hey, look who decided to show," Tom said. "Better hurry. If Coach Nelson hits the ice before you do, you'll be skating laps when the rest of us are in the dining hall."

I can put my skates on fairly quickly, but that day I think I must have broken some kind of boot-lacing record. I changed out my everyday glasses for the heavy-duty, black-framed ones, and then I was in the corridor, walking on the rubber mat, heading up the short ramp. There was the ice, glowing like some great white jewel, with a trace of mist hanging on it, and that cold, clean smell filled my lungs, and suddenly I knew that everything would be all right. The other boys (about twenty of them, I guess) were getting loose, some of them stretching against the boards, some skating figure-eights in the face-off circles. I spotted Rocky Lufrano right away, practicing little cutting moves around the net, and once again I had the funny feeling that I had met him before - his skating style was so familiar. Clark Hightower came over and banged my shin guards with his stick.

"You ready?" he asked, grinning around his yellow mouthpiece. I nodded. From behind me came the shriek of a whistle and a booming voice: "All right, four laps and then everybody on the red line. Right now!"

That was the first time I heard the voice that I would come to know so well. When Coach Nelson yelled, it was like a cross between a dog barking and someone singing out of tune, and it always caught me off guard and made me jump a little. Naturally I had heard my dad yell a lot, as my coach, but it never seemed like yelling. And I always understood every word he said when I was out on the ice, but with Coach Nelson it was sometimes hard to hear. To be fair, of course, I was just used to my dad, and Coach Nelson was never mean, after all, and he certainly did know the game of hockey. And as he made very clear to us that first day that he had no time for any goofing around.

When we were all lined up across the red line and breathing hard, he said, "Boys, this is where it all begins. If we work hard now, and continue to do so, we can repeat as district champs. And what with the new talent we have, I see no reason we shouldn't go all the way to states."

He looked us up and down and nodded. He was not a big man at all, but tough-looking, like Jim, the mechanic who worked on our car in Port Royal. "Is Gibbs here?" Coach Nelson asked.

"Right here, Coach," I said.

"Good. Step up here a minute, son. Boys, this is Gil Gibbs. He's just coming into the seventh grade here. He's come all the way from Maine, and I want you all to make him feel welcome."

I thought I heard Rocky mutter something under his breath, but I couldn't be sure. He was looking straight ahead. I wondered what his idea of making me feel "welcome" would be.

Practice was good, but it really wasn't any tougher than anything I'd done in Port Royal. Overall, I guess these kids were slightly better skaters than most I had known, and certainly they were bigger. As we went through the typical drills - stickhandling, passing, three-on-twos and so on - I was impressed with Rock's play. He was really fluid, and he carried himself in a neat package that seemed ready to explode at any time. After about a half-hour of drills, Coach Nelson got out a bag of red vests, and he called out some lines for a scrimmage. As it turned out, I was playing left defenseman on Rocky Lufrano's line. The only other guys I knew, Tom and Clark, were forwards on the other side, but I quickly learned the others' names: Brent and Mike and Dustin and the rest as they called out to one another on the ice.

It didn't take long for the action to get hot. Lufrano and I worked well together, as I hit him once with a pass off of the boards as he slipped into the slot. One little flick and it was in, the back of the net quivering in that old familiar way. He skated over to me and we high-fived with our gloves. I thought, this kid's okay after all... but I still could have sworn that I'd met him someplace before.

It was pretty even after that. Tom and Clark were pretty good players, too, and once Tom beat me on a breakaway because I couldn't get turned and stumbled over myself, and he took it, and the puck ricocheted off the far post and in. I looked over at Rocky, expecting a reprimand from him, but he just shook his head and said, "Let it go, man." Bailey, however, was not as inclined to let it go. He skated close to me, grinning good-naturedly.

"And the Cruncher lights the light!" he shouted. "Just listen to that crowd... Crunch! Crunch! Crunch!" He pointed his finger at me, but I knew he was just kidding around. It was a similar play, though, just a few minutes later, when the bad thing happened.

Tom Bailey, my roommate, was barreling down at me again along the boards, and I was determined not to let him get past me this time. I skated straight at him, digging at his stick with mine and trying just to ease him off the puck with my hip, but at the last moment he backhanded it off of the glass and it squirted out onto the open ice. From the corner of my eye I saw a figure in red speeding towards us. The explosion missed me altogether, and it took a second or two for me to understand what had happened: the impact of Rocky's body check had carried Tom backward a full ten feet, and he struck the boards with the back of his head and his shoulders. By the time I got over to him, several other boys were already standing around him, staring down in

stunned silence. Coach Nelson, who really hadn't said much of anything thus far, made his way over and knelt down by Tom.

"You all right, Bailey?"

"I... I think so, Coach," Tom said. "Just my head hurts a little."

"All right, all right, boys. He's okay. Mike, Brent, help me get him up. The rest of you, hit the showers. Lufrano, I'd like to see you in my office as soon as possible." As we were leaving the ice, it was as if the others didn't know what to say to Rocky, whether to hate him or to congratulate him on what was probably the best and hardest check any of us had ever seen. Clark Hightower was the one exception.

"Hey, Lufrano. You think it's cool to try and take out your own teammate?"

"Ah, put a cork in it, Hightower. This is hockey, not ballet."

"What you did was unnecessary. If I were you, I'd be looking over my own shoulder."

Rocky said nothing else, but quietly went to his locker and began removing his gear. "I've had about enough of that guy," Clark said. "He'll get his one of these days."

Tom was all right, after all. He made it to the dining hall, looking a little sheepish and embarrassed as he stood in the serving line. He even kidded himself about it a little:

"Crunch gets crunched," he said. Rocky sat across the room with a couple of the older players. He didn't smile or joke.

After dinner I was making my way across the quad, wondering what my family would be eating back home. I hoped it wasn't Mom's baked chicken and stuffing, because I hated to think I might be missing out on that. Afterwards little Rose would be out in the backyard, maybe in the treehouse with a couple of her friends; that kid loves to be outdoors as much as I do. And Dad would retire to his den to mess around with his stereo and his jazz records. The wind in the treetops made me think of my bedroom at night, where I could watch the shadows of the limbs scramble around on the wall when the moon was behind them. It wasn't scary, not even at Halloween, and it always made me feel safe to think that those trees had been there for a long, long time. Walking along, I had made myself good and homesick when I heard a voice calling softly to me.

"Hey, Gil..." A dark figure emerged from the doorway of the library and came toward me. It was Rocky. His face looked odd – his brow was all knitted up.

"Hi, Rock," I said.

"I just wanted to know... Are the guys saying things about me? Bad things, I mean?"

"Well... no, Rock. At least, I didn't hear anything."

"I didn't mean to hurt Bailey, you know. I was just trying to prevent another goal."

I shrugged my shoulders. "Like you said, it's a contact sport. Besides, he wasn't really hurt."

"That's good."

We headed toward the dormitory. "Say," I said. "What did Coach have to say to you? Was he ticked about that hit?"

Rocky shook his head vigorously. "Oh, no, not at all. In fact, he talked about you. He wants us to work together a lot more. Said he sees a lot of potential there. Wants us to work on a deflection play, stuff like that."

"I've never played defense before," I said.

"You looked good out there today. Coach said so."

"Thanks."

So it was that the Rocky I knew, beginning with that night, was perhaps different from the boy other people saw. I wasn't sure how his reputation had gone so sour. I figured that the incident last year, with Tom Bailey's old roommate, must have been unintentional. Sure, Rocky played rough, but this was hockey. He was just quiet, was all, and didn't really speak up to defend himself or apologize.

Whoever he was, he was a much more complicated kid than anyone had given him credit for. He was to prove that to me, time and time again.

Chapter Four
A Figure in Black

It didn't take me long to realize that there was a lot more to life at the Price School for Boys than playing hockey. I attended six classes a day, with a half-hour squeezed in to wolf down lunch, and I was also expected to join a school activity (I signed up to write for the school's online newspaper, the *Panther's Call*). Then there was practice (I still had not even had the time to stop and examine the trophies and pictures in the lobby of the arena; that's how hectic things were). Plus, after practice and dinner each evening, we were required to attend study hall in the library, so that by the time I got back to my room, my clock-radio's red numerals would read 9:30. And I was usually so tired by then that those numbers were the last thing I'd remember.

Still, I am very fond of the place, and I like thinking about those times. Hockey players do a lot of horsing around, you see, and the Panthers were no exception. For instance, an awful lot of shaving cream got used up that year, even though most of us were not old enough to shave: I learned to check near the bottom of my sheets each night before I put my feet in. And one morning, when I was in a real hurry to make it to a science test, Bailey and Hightower switched my blazer with one belonging to Bobby Horner, the smallest guy on the team at seventy-five pounds. I actually went to class squeezed into that tiny jacket, wondering if I could have grown that much overnight, but when I saw Horner sitting in the back of the room, his little face barely visible in my blazer, I figured things out.

And then there was the time someone sawed halfway through the blade of Hightower's hockey stick, down near the heel, so that the first time he took a slapshot the handle came right off in his hands. The blade went straight into the goal, but the puck didn't. And we all had a good laugh out of it, but Clark didn't. We never knew who pulled that one, but I suspected Tom Bailey was paying him back for having short-sheeted his bunk the week before. Besides, when it happened, it was Bailey who said,

"Guess you should switch to a carbon blade, Clark."

Even though they didn't realize it, those fellows also helped me to understand how different a place Maine really is from anywhere else. I simply didn't seem to see the world in quite the same way they did; I don't really know how to explain it except to say that folks in my hometown are a little less complicated, somehow – simpler, but in a very good way. Some might think them gruffer, maybe, but that's because we all come from working stock. My dad teaches math at the high school, but his father was a millworker and a lumberman, and so was my mom's. It took me a while even to catch on to the good-natured teasing those Price School guys (who were mostly from New Hampshire and Massachusetts) aimed at me: for instance, in evening study hall, if I asked Bailey what page the English homework was on, he would stab at my book with a finger and rasp, "It's right theyah, Mainah! Can't you see it?" and the other boys would clap their hands over their mouths to contain their giggling, but I'd be wondering what was so funny.

I have to admit that Price School academics were tough. I'd always done pretty well at Port Royal's schools, but that didn't prepare me for the workload I had at Price. I was relieved at the six-weeks grading period to have B's in everything except science, in which I got an A-. But the class I liked the most was history, and I can't really say why. I just like learning about the people who lived a long time ago, in the same way, I guess, that my dad likes those old jazz records. Some things get better as time goes on, he says, but some don't. And my history teacher, Mr. Birnham, was a great guy, and he was the whole reason, really, that I signed up for the newspaper, since he was also the advisor. He had a slogan written on poster-board and taped up over the newspaper office door: *Seek the truth and present it fairly.* I liked that.

The only one who seemed apart from everything was Rocky Lufrano. He went where the other boys went, ate when we ate, hit the books when we did (in fact, he was a straight-A student), and he also was a member of the Outdoors Club... but he was different somehow. He didn't take part in our discussions or laugh at our jokes. I could never quite figure out whether he felt he was too mature for us or else he really didn't have anything to say, but I have to admit he did a lot of talking on the ice - not with words but with his skating, his stickhandling, and his checking, which we all respected more and more with each practice. He seemed to be more comfortable around adults: I saw him many times on campus with Mr. Withers, to whom I'd hardly spoken since arriving at Price that first day, and also sitting in the metal chair in Coach Nelson's office. The rest of us knew that if we ever ended up sitting there, it was because we had done something wrong. Not true with Rocky - he sometimes went in just to hang out.

I suppose I probably talked with him more than just about anybody else on the team. He was more at ease with me for some reason, and once or twice, on weekends before the season started, he asked me to join the Outdoors Club on their hikes through the woods around the school. Rocky tended to open up a bit out there, and he told me that he had used to go hunting with his dad quite a lot before he'd gone away to boarding school. I guess it made him feel a little better to be out there among the trees, with their yellow and red leaves and his thoughts of his father.

Of course, we were all looking forward to our first hockey game of the season. It came soon enough, in mid-October, and it was like nothing else I'd experienced before.

The crowds at Peewee League games had always been small, mostly the relatives of the kids who were playing, and even most of our travel team's games, once I started playing in the bantam division, were sparsely attended. Price School games, as I soon found out, were events attended by the whole student body, the faculty, and the principal, and even some grown-ups who had gone to Price. I sure was glad that our first contest was a home game - it felt good hearing everybody cheering us on. When we hit the ice in our red and yellow jerseys... well, as I said already, it was like nothing else I'd experienced before.

I played on the first line as left defenseman. Truly, I hadn't caught on to defense yet, but I was usually able to use my speed to make up for my mistakes. The team we played was a public middle school from Portsmouth, and we handled them easily, 5-2. Rocky had a hat trick, and Clark Hightower scored our other two, and I was pleased because I had an assist on one of Rocky's goals, a deflection, the play we had been working on so much in practice.

The deflection is one of the hardest things to do in hockey. Someone puts a shot down along the ice, and a forward who has planted himself in front of the goal just tips it into the net. It's hard because the pass is usually made through traffic, and the forward must also try to block the goalie's vision, or screen him. Rocky and I got to be pretty good at it. Before long I could put the puck right on the tape of his stick's blade, and he would re-direct it, turning the blade just slightly one way or the other to send the puck rocketing into the corner of the net. It was just like the pros do it.

We were even better at it in our second game of the year, against Fraley Catholic, another boarding school. Those guys were big - I was checked pretty hard a couple of times - but Rocky and I combined for two more deflections and we won 2-0. It was all fine: Mr. Birnham came to watch, and Mr. Withers, but the best part of all was that my dad came down from Port Royal to see me play (my mom couldn't make it because little Rose had a fever), and he took me out to dinner afterwards. It was strange, really, because it was the first time he had been at a game of mine where he wasn't coaching. He would smile and wave at me, though, each time I skated out onto the ice, and he seemed okay with it, so I played extra hard to prove I was okay with it, too. I had a couple of nice plays on defense, if I do say so myself, catching the big Fraley center from behind once and saving a sure goal another time by covering the open side of the net and flicking the puck back up the boards.

I felt really good when my dad and I sat down to dinner, better than I had in a long time, to be truthful. It was a sort of dark, quiet restaurant, with candles on the tables, and my hair was still wet from the shower. Dad smiled and talked a lot, filling me in on everything that was happening back home, although I could tell he was making an extra special effort to make me feel as though everything was fine. Looking back on it, though, I realize it must have been hard for him, because he always loved coaching me. I knew that he still coached the same youth team back in Port Royal, but I can just imagine how lonely that was for him, going out to the rink every day and coming home by himself. Now I know that was something I couldn't have seen any other way.

It's hard to explain, but being away from home really made me think about many things from another point of view. If I didn't learn anything else, at least I learned that.

But on this night, at dinner after our big win over Fraley, my dad and I had a good time. "How do you like it playing defense?" he asked.

I swallowed a mouthful of baked potato. "Oh, I like it. It's a bit rougher back there. I think I'm picking up a lot of stuff I didn't know before."

"You can never learn enough about the game. There's always something more to know. Do you remember when you were five and six years old? I had you playing defenseman sometimes back then."

"Yes, I do. It's helping me an awful lot." That wasn't entirely true; I didn't remember much about it. Of course, I had always played hockey, but I don't suppose I cared much back then what my position was. I just wanted to be on the ice, anyplace on the ice. I wanted to glide.

"Think Coach Nelson will use you at forward this season?" Dad asked.

"Gee, I don't know. We've got plenty of good forwards, you know. And things are working well with Rocky and me on the first line..."

"That's true enough. He's a good player, that Rocky. Got size, speed... all the tools."

I was silent for a bit. Then I said, "Dad, what do you think about a kid who plays that well but doesn't seem to like his teammates very much?"

He weighed the question carefully. "I don't know. I suppose hockey players are like anybody else. You've really

43

got to get to know them before you say much about them. This Rocky... does he not get along well on the team?"

"It's not that. He's just always off by himself. Don't know how to take him, really."

"Hm. Give him a chance, is what I always say. But you know me, son - I'd always rather have a team player than a guy who only goes for himself."

I nodded. That was the trouble, though. I didn't get the feeling that Rocky only went for himself. But he didn't seem to care about the team, either. Just play hockey, I told myself. You don't have to make friends with the guy.

Anyway, my dad and I had an awesome time together. We didn't talk hockey at all the rest of the night. He told me a funny story about our neighbor, Mr. Jonas Smalkey, who had gone out to get the morning paper and been chased down the street in his bathrobe by his own dog, Heckler. Then he told me about Rose and how she had refused to admit she was sick even after the school nurse had sent her home on Friday with a 102-degree temperature. She's about as stubborn as I am, I guess.

So we talked and talked and ate and ate, and we had a fine time. I was sad to see him leave. I walked up to my dorm room and opened the blinds and watched the old Bel-Air drive away, and as I was watching, I saw something strange. I was about to close the blinds and go to bed, but I caught a glimpse of a figure in black just coming around the corner of the library. I squinted, and recognized the rolling gait: it was Rocky Lufrano. The strange thing was, there's nothing beyond the library at Price except for a couple of academic buildings - the science and math wings - and some teachers' offices. Beyond that is woods. I couldn't imagine what he had been doing over there at that hour.

It was really a mystery. And had I been able to solve it then, I could have saved myself a whole lot of trouble.

Chapter Five

Two Dreams and One Nightmare

"All right, Gil, let's win this face-off!"

I looked up toward the voice. It was the same one I had always heard in this situation, in many other games just like this one. My team was in a 2-2 tie with less than one minute remaining. What the voice was really saying to me was: Remember all that you've worked so hard for, decide whether you really want to win, and then get the job done. Now was the time.

I dug in with the edges of my skates and focused on the faded pink face-off dot. I was winded and breathing heavily, and my clear plastic face shield had a streak of water across it, where ice had been kicked up in the preceding scramble. I was deep in my own defensive zone, and I could see the goalie, crouched and rigid, from the corner of my eye. It was true: I had to win this face-off.

The puck came down hard, and when I saw it, I thrust my shoulder into the opposing center and pushed, feeling him teeter off-balance. At the same time, as the puck struck the ice and bounced, I scooped it in the curve of my blade, flicking it between my own legs to the right wing. Then we were off, skating side by side and splitting up and around the last blue-sweatered defenseman, with the left wing trailing in an all-out sprint to the goal. The right wing skidded the puck back to me as we closed in, and I had time for one quick head fake before I took my shot. It was enough: the puck whizzed in just over the goalie's glove, and the back of the net shivered like a spider's web when you touch it. Our players' sticks went into the air all at once like flags.

"Atta' way, Gil!" my father shouted from the box. "Gil!! Hey, Gil!"

"Hey, Gil! Wake up, Gil!"

It was Tom Bailey's voice now. I had been dreaming that I was back in Port Royal, playing for my dad's team again. Suddenly the reality of morning washed over me. It was Saturday, and the Price School Panthers had an away game. It was to be a long trip, four hours on the road through the White Mountains, and we had to catch the bus by eight in order to get there by lunchtime. The game was set for two o'clock. Bailey was dressed in jeans and a sweater. At least we wouldn't have to wear coats and ties today, I thought. I had really had a tough time getting used to that - especially the tie. Sometimes I felt like I would surely choke.

I got dressed quickly and then put my hockey gear, which I had left hanging over the closet door to air out, into the big black bag, with the skates in the end compartments. Then I put my two sticks, the old aluminum one and my new, one-piece carbon stick, into my stick bag, and followed Tom out the door, through the hallway, down the echoing stairwell, and out into the crisp October morning. We dropped our gear on the sidewalk beside the dormitory and then made our way to the dining hall.

The team was somber, still half-asleep. One thing I've learned is that no matter how good a school is, somehow the food is never very tasty. I wouldn't say that the Price meals were bad, exactly... just sort of bland. And the dining room itself always had a heavy smell, especially in the fall and winter when the big windows fogged up, like years and years worth of steam and grease. This morning I tried to play it safe with some pancakes and fruit, but I felt so tired it hardly mattered. All the players seemed to be in a similar state, and

Coach Nelson must have sensed it the moment he walked in, because he said,

"You guys had better wake up. This team we're playing today shouldn't be taken lightly. They were Northern Region champs last year. Now let's finish up with breakfast and get on the bus."

As we slowly dieseled down the drive and then swung awkwardly up onto the highway, nobody talked. I couldn't figure out what it was. Maybe we were all tired from so much schoolwork and hockey practice, not to mention doing our own laundry and seeing to all the details of life at a boarding school. I realized that even though I was making out all right, and even though I had been fairly independent back home anyway, this was a tremendous change for me. In a way I wished that bus would head straight for Port Royal and drop me off right in front of my own house. My mom and dad would probably be in the breakfast room, reading the paper and drinking coffee. My little sister Rose would be outside already, playing some game with her friends from down the street, but she would come running when she saw me. She's always interested in whatever I'm doing, and she would have a hundred questions for me about school and hockey and everything else.

That's what I was thinking when I fell asleep on the bus, but I didn't dream about home this time. It was eerie: I dreamt the lawn at Price had turned all to ice, but my skates were too big for me and I was stumbling along, trying to make it to science class on time. The funny thing was it was still dark, and the lights were on in all the buildings. And way off in the distance I could see Rocky Lufrano, dressed in black, with a black hockey stick, and he was shooting pucks at me. I didn't know whether to get out of the way of the pucks as they came zipping at my head, or to try and stop them. Then Coach Nelson was yelling at me: "Come on, Gibbs! You've got to stop his shot!" I wanted to ask Coach how come Rocky was shooting on his own teammate, but when I turned around, there was no one there. I snapped my head back again just in time to see the figure in black hit a slap shot that sent a puck screaming right at me, and I tried to duck. I must have really jumped, because I woke myself up. Clark Hightower, who was sitting next to me in the bus seat, said, 'Geez, Gil, what's wrong? I didn't know whether to wake you or not."

"Just a dream," I mumbled. "...Thank goodness."

Once we had arrived at New Hampton, we got our lunches out of two big boxes - more cafeteria food, ham sandwiches this time. I hated lounging around that way before the game; I think it added to the feeling of drowsiness we all seemed to share.

And once the game did finally get underway, from the very opening face-off, I knew that things would not go well. The ice at New Hampton was like mush, but their players seemed to be used to it, beating us to the puck on almost every rush. And they had the size advantage, too, with big, thick-legged forwards and hard-checking defensemen, so that every place I looked, it seemed, I saw a grey and gold New Hampton sweater. At the end of the first period, the score was 2-0 in their favor.

Coach Nelson had very little to say to us in the locker room, except for a few adjustments; even he seemed about to accept defeat. I looked up at the others, all seated on the benches with their heads down and their sticks between their legs.

"C'mon, fellas," I said. "These guys aren't that good."

Only Rocky Lufrano looked over at me, but he shook his head. His eyes seemed to say, It's just not our day. We had been undefeated coming in, five wins and no losses. Today's game was not a district game, so we would remain in first place, but I had taken to emailing my dad after each victory and raving about the team (maybe overdoing it a little, to make him think I wasn't all that homesick), and now it seemed I would have to tone things down considerably. Too, next weekend we would play a school not far from Port Royal, and I knew my family would probably come out to watch, so I had good reason to hope we could snap out of our slump by then. What a nightmare this trip had turned out to be.

In a game like that, sometimes you get a lift from the most unlikely guy. I still remember my first goal. I was only six, playing with mostly eight year-olds, and we were really getting blown away in that one: it was 9-0 late in the third period. I intercepted a pass, squirted through the defense, and took a shot on goal, lifting the puck as I had never been able to do before. It went in. That was our only goal that day, but I'll never forget it. Well, against New Hampton, it was little Bobby Horner who shone for the Panthers. With about three minutes to go, he skated around two of the big grey and gold-shirted goons, went in behind the net, stopped short and wrapped the puck on the same side he'd gone in. It was a beautiful and intelligent play, and the New Hampton goalie never knew what hit him.

But that was it for us. We lost 4-1, and the ride back home was no fun at all, but of course, now I was wide awake. I wished that I could go to sleep and forget the whole day, but all I could do was stare out the bus's window as twilight fell over the White Mountains. It was still only November, but this was a winter sky - ash grey with streaks of yellow through it. We ought to be getting our first snowfall before too long, I thought. My father and I had a tradition at Thanksgiving: if there was snow, we got out our cross-country skis and my grandfather's old cross-cut saw, and we would journey beyond the hill above Port Royal, scouting for a Christmas tree. The land was owned by a friend of my dad's, and so it was all right. Usually we could find a good tree, not too big, so that we could drag it along behind us. We would put it in the garage, where the snow and ice stuck to it would melt away, and on Friday we would shape it and then set it up in the living room, and we would all begin the trimming of it, with the smell of pine and of winter in the house with us. I wasn't certain, but I think the Panthers were scheduled to play in a tournament over the Thanksgiving weekend. I began to feel homesick again.

Back on campus, after dinner and study hall, some of the boys rode into town with Coach Nelson and Mr. Withers to see a movie. I guess the idea was to make us feel better after the nightmare in New Hampton. But I stayed in.

Most of the guys on the team – and for that matter, most of the students at Price – had their own cellphones, and were in the habit of texting. My parents had already decided that I didn't need my own cell, however, since there was a telephone in my dorm's lounge, and I was allowed to use that one anytime I chose. Besides, they were right: although I'd been awarded a scholarship to go to Price, my family still had lots of other expenses to worry about. So, I sat by the window with my laptop and began my email:

> *Dear Dad,*
> *Well, we did not have our best game today...*

Once I got into it, though, it wasn't all that hard to write. There could be worse things, I thought, than losing a hockey game. At least, that was probably what my dad would have said...

Chapter Six
A Mystery Solved

It was a couple of weeks later that Rocky began to show signs of warming up to me. I'm still not sure why he began to like me - especially after everything else that happened - but for some reason, he began to wait for me outside the locker room after practice, to sit with me and Bailey and Hightower at meals, and even to stop by our dorm rooms in the evenings. Much later on, Tom and Clark said I was a fool not to see that Rocky was just using me, but I still believe there was more to it than that. I think that in some way, we connected.

For instance, I'll never forget the weekend just before the Thanksgiving break. Bailey's parents had come up that Saturday and taken him out to dinner. It was around eight, and I had nowhere to go, and so I opened up my history book to catch up on some reading and start preparing for a big chapter test in Mr. Birnham's class. There was a knock on the door, and Rock came strolling in, and suddenly, seeing him in profile, I had the odd feeling once again that I had seen him someplace before, long before I had even heard of the Price School.

He sat down on Bailey's bed. "Hey. You've got Birnham for history, don't you?"

"Yeah," I said.

"Me, too. Big test coming up, huh?"

"Yeah. It takes me a while to get ready. I don't catch on real quick in history, but I like it. I like Mr. Birnham, I mean."

"He's okay," Rocky said. He looked around the room at Bailey's posters and stuff. For a minute I was a little embarrassed that I had admitted liking Mr. Birnham's class. A lot of the guys pretended to hate their teachers, you see. But I did like him, and he had encouraged me a good deal with my writing for the newspaper, had even given me my own sports column, in which I wrote not only about the school's athletics but also about professional hockey, football, baseball... whatever I wanted. It was one of my favorite things about Price.

"Well... we can study for the history test together if you want," I offered.

"Huh? Oh, no thanks. I've already got it covered."

I closed the book and set it on the desk. "Can't concentrate," I said.

"Hey, what do you guys do for fun on Saturday nights up in Port Royal?" Rocky asked.

"Not much. If there's no hockey going on, we might go bowling. Or have some neighbors over maybe. You know, small town stuff. Play baseball in the summer."

Rocky nodded. "Spend a lot of time with your dad, do you?"

"Yeah, a pretty good amount. How about you?"

His eyes wandered around the room again. "Used to," he said.

There was an awkward silence, which I tried to fill: "What happened? Did he just get busy at work?"

Now Rocky looked at the floor. "Yeah. I guess so. Plus, I didn't really want to come to Price. I wanted to go to the local school. But my dad wanted me to play hockey here. See, my brother played here. He's a big-time college player now."

"No kidding? What's your brother's name?"

"Benny Lufrano."

It was like waking up from a deep sleep. Suddenly I realized where I had seen Rocky before - rather, it wasn't him I had seen; it was his brother. I had seen his face many times, in fact, in the *Port Royal Lantern*, our newspaper back home. He was a star player at the University of Maine and was in his senior year. He would probably win the Hobey Baker Award this season and was a shoo-in for the National Hockey League...

"Benny Lufrano," I said. "Didn't he lead the nation in scoring last season?"

Rocky nodded. "Not only that. He's an academic All-American. He was always on the Headmaster's List here at Price. Once he got to high school at St. Paul Prep, same deal. My dad thinks I ought to be just like him."

"Wow," I said. "Benny Lufrano. Incredible. It wouldn't be so bad to be like Benny Lufrano."

"You're right. Unless you're his kid brother. Then everybody *expects* you to be like him. But what if you're not as good?"

"But you are good. You're a good student, too."

He shook his head. "Not good enough. Not good enough for my dad."

"Well, maybe your dad should lighten up. Hockey is supposed to be fun."

"The bad thing is, I remember when it was fun. We were little, and Benny and I used to go to the pond down the street from our house. Dad played, too. Nobody ever talked about college scholarships or grades or the Price School. Benny was the greatest... he still is. He always looked out for me and helped me with my skates when I was little, stuff like that."

"You're from Massachusetts, though, aren't you? How'd your brother end up at Maine?"

"Our family has a long history there. My dad played there, too, way back before the Black Bears were even any good. And they gave Benny a full ride."

"Come to think of it," I said. "It would be great being Benny Lufrano's brother. But I can see how it would be pretty tough, too."

"It's tough, all right. I know that the alumni and Mr. Withers and Coach Nelson and everybody on the team expect me to be as good as him."

"It's funny," I said. "'I've never heard anybody on the team say anything about it. I doubt that the other guys know about Benny."

"Oh, they know, all right. They all know. They just don't talk about it, but they know."

He got up, walked over and picked up my stick, which was leaning in the corner. He took two or three imaginary wrist shots, and I could hear the whoosh as the blade was whipped through the air. "Hey," he said. "I've been meaning to tell you. You're a good defensive player. I think we've been really clicking on that deflection play."

"Thanks. That's a good play. You're pretty quick in front of the net." He grinned for the first time since he had come in the room.

"Well," he said. "Gotta go."

"Okay. See you."

"Right."

I resumed my quiet Saturday night. But I had learned more about Rocky Lufrano and the history of hockey at the Price School in twenty minutes than I had in the previous two months. It was no small deal being Benny Lufrano's brother. I wondered why I had never heard about it.

Bailey set me straight on all of that when he came back from dinner with his parents. "OF COURSE, we don't talk about it," he said. "Nobody talks about it. But Benny's name is plastered all over the trophy case in the arena lobby. I don't understand why you haven't noticed. Don't you wear your glasses all the time?"

I remembered myself rushing past that trophy case to get to practice day after day. I guess I haven't exactly taken the time to look," I said.

"Gotta take the time," Bailey said. "Gotta pay attention. Gotta know what's up."

I had wandered over to the window. The trees were practically bare, except for a stand of evergreens above the history wing. I felt like an idiot not to have known about Rocky's brother, but now everything had fallen into place... I remembered when I was coming up in the Squirts division back in Port Royal: Hank Greer, our team's big center, had moved away, and I knew I would have to try and fill his shoes - or fill his skates, to be more accurate. It wasn't long before everyone had forgotten about Hank, but Rocky could never forget about Benny; brothers are forever, I guess.

As I looked out over the campus, something moved in the shadows. Someone was walking, not along the walkway but behind the hedge that ran beside it, toward the classroom buildings. It was the figure in black again - unmistakably, it was Rocky. His walk was really sort of awkward, now that I thought of it, with none of the instinctive grace he showed on skates.

"Hey, Tom, check this out," I said.

Bailey came to the window. "Who could that be, at this time of night? It's almost midnight."

"It's Rocky," I whispered.

He studied the figure. "You're right. What do you think he's up to?"

"I don't know," I said, "but I'm going to find out." I took my jacket off the hook on the back of the door.

"Hey, wait a minute, Gil. You'd better think about this first. It's obvious that whatever Rocky is up to, he doesn't want anyone to know about it. Maybe you'd better let him alone."

"I think he was pretty depressed when he left here," I said. "What are teammates for, right? Besides, I'm curious, aren't you?"

Bailey shook his head. "It doesn't pay to be too curious sometimes. Let it go."

"It'll be okay, roomie." I was out the door and heading down the hallway before he had a chance to say anything else.

Many times since that night, though, I've wondered if maybe Tom Bailey was right after all.

Chapter Seven
The End of Something

It was chilly outside, so I started to trot. As I jogged past the floodlights along the walkway, I watched my shadow race ahead of me and then fall gradually behind. For just a moment, the whole thing struck me as so strange: what was I doing here, so far from Port Royal, out at this time of night? But then I saw Rocky at the side of the history building; he took a quick look over his shoulder, then opened the janitor's door and slipped inside, and I knew then that I had to find out what he was doing here.

I crept in the thick shadow of the building, through the janitor's closet, and found myself in the hallway of the history building. It was very dark, except for a flickering light that seemed to come from Mr. Birnham's classroom. It was eerie in here at night, and I paused for what must have been two or three minutes, listening to my own breath and wondering if maybe I should forget this and go back to the dorm and get some sleep. But I'd come this far; there was no turning back.

I walked softly down the hall, past the school newspaper's office, with the sign over the door saying, *Seek the truth and present it fairly.* I stopped in Mr. Birnham's doorway. I saw Rocky seated at the teacher's desk, with his flashlight trained downward on some papers he was removing from a drawer. Then he muttered something, placed one set of papers on the desk, and began to study them closely.

On impulse, I reached over and turned on the classroom's lights, and the sudden brilliance made me squint.

Rocky didn't jump, but quickly looked up at me. "You idiot!" he rasped. "Turn those lights off!"

"What are you doing, Rocky?" I really hadn't understood yet.

"What do you think I'm doing? I'm looking for a copy of the history test we're taking on Monday. Now, for the last time, turn those lights off, unless you want to get us both kicked out of school."

But as it all sank in, somehow I knew it was too late already. A sense of doom hung in the air as we looked at one another, and then I heard the security guard's voice behind me:

"All right, boys. Let's go. You've got some explaining to do."

And then I heard the rustling of the guard's nylon jacket as he placed his hand on my shoulder, but my eyes were locked on Rocky's, and now I saw an outpouring of such hatred that it sent a chill through me. I tried to speak, to say that it wasn't me, that I didn't belong here in the first place, but the words wouldn't come out.

Rocky flicked off the flashlight and slid the desk drawer shut with a hollow sound.

It really is a blur, everything else that happened that night. I remember Mr. Birnham in a gray sweatshirt and blue jeans, with the shadow of a beard, and Mr. Withers, who walked over from his house next door to Price, sitting there in his bathrobe and staring straight at Rocky through his gold spectacles. We sat in chairs in the principal's office, although the principal didn't show up; Mr. Withers sat at his desk, and after what seemed like an eternity, he asked:

"Do you boys know the Price School's policy concerning cheating?"

Rocky looked down at the rug and nodded.

Another eternity, and Mr. Withers asked, "Is there any possible explanation for what you've done, other than the obvious one?"

I tried to speak: "I..."

"Yes, Gibbs?"

"I... didn't... I mean..." I looked over at Rock, but he was still staring downward. "I didn't cheat, Mr. Withers. Ask Rocky."

He turned his gaze back to my teammate. "Lufrano? Do you have anything to say in defense of Mr. Gibbs here?"

A painful minute crept by, and then he did it: Rocky shook his head no. And suddenly I saw my future before me, beginning with the telephone call I would have to make to my parents and then the long car ride back to Port Royal and the ruined holidays, and on and on.

"Well, all right, then," Mr. Withers said. "We'll hold an emergency hearing before the honor council tomorrow morning at 8:00 sharp, and then decide on the appropriate punishments. You boys can return to your dormitories. I advise you to get some sleep."

Of course, sleeping was impossible. I laid there in the dark and told Tom Bailey the whole story, and then after a little while he said,

"So Rocky wouldn't back you up, eh? I might have known. Well, don't worry. I'll go to that meeting, too, and tell the truth about what happened. They'll have to listen. Geez, Gil, I told you not to go after him in the dark."

"Too late now," I said. "What am I going to tell my dad?"

"Let's see how it goes in the morning. Maybe you won't have to tell him anything."

"You know, it's funny. I think, in a way, Rocky wanted to get caught. He's never been happy here, you know. It was just unlucky that he pulled me down with him. Like a drowning victim, I guess."

"Hey, nobody's drowned yet. Let's see how it goes."

After a while, Tom's breathing grew steady and deep, and I knew he was asleep. But I got up and went to the window and looked out at the dark line of evergreens and then the scraggly, bare limbs in the other direction, and I had a feeling that things would not turn out so well. I must have stood there for a long time, because pretty soon the first pink shades of morning seeped in under the branches, and I looked over at the clock. Six-thirty. Could it be that all of this was just a bad dream? But when I looked out again, I saw the same security guard making his last rounds in the pink and grey dawning, and I knew it had all really happened. I went to the closet and took out my navy blue Price School blazer and hung it on the door handle.

Then I grabbed my towel and headed down the hallway for the showers.

"It was a cold Sunday in mid-November."

Sometimes I pretend that my life is a story, and that those words are the beginning of a very important though unhappy chapter. But it passes quickly, with the sound of footsteps in a hallway, a blur of stern adult faces and official words, and then my own voice, speaking in my own defense, and then the voices of other boys and then more stern words from the adults, and then footsteps in the hallway again, and the chapter is over. And I feel a sense of relief.

Relief that it is over. Rocky Lufrano and I were expelled from the Price School for honor code violations - cheating on a history test, to be exact. The honor council, made up of three of the best eighth grade students and three

teachers, judged that we were both guilty, despite Tom
Bailey's argument, on my behalf, that I had followed Rocky
that night out of personal concern for him, with no intent to
cheat. I can understand that, though. The council probably
figured that a guy's roommate would lie to try and save him.
They had to base their decision on the facts, they said, and
the facts were not in my favor. We should be grateful, they
said, that we had not been charged with breaking and
entering as well.

When they asked Rocky about it, he at least told a half-
truth. "I'm not sure why Gibbs was there," he said. "I turned
around and he was standing there. That's all I remember."

I could not meet the eyes of Mr. Birnham or Mr.
Withers, who were both present again. I felt I couldn't face
their disappointment in me. Coach Nelson was there, too, and
he made a brave speech about my character and Rocky's
character, and he told them that we were actually fine young
men who had perhaps made a mistake, and would make up
for it in our value to the school. I'm sure he was thinking
mostly about the Thanksgiving Tournament coming up that
week. It was a good speech, it really was. But it was not
enough. We were to call our parents, explain what had

happened, and then pack our things and depart from the Price School that afternoon.

I expected calling home to be the hardest part of all, and it was. I talked to my dad first, speaking slowly in the beginning but then letting the words rush out of me. I don't know what I was scared of, because when I finished, saying, "I didn't do it, Dad," he said,

"I know you didn't, Gil. I'll drive over right away. Maybe I can talk to Mr. Withers."

My mom got on the phone, then. She was crying. "It's all right, Gil. Don't worry. Whatever happens, it'll be all right."

"Okay, Mom." But I felt really awful. There's hardly anything worse than making your mother cry.

My dad did talk to Mr. Withers, but all he would say was that we should write a letter and that maybe the administration would review the case in a week or so, after things settled down a bit. For now, though, we must abide by the council's decision, he said.

Dad pulled the Bel-Air around to the dorm, and Tom Bailey helped me pack my stuff. Neither of us felt like talking. I carefully put my sticks in their bag, and I slipped the blade guards on my skates before stowing them. Just in case, I packed up all my textbooks, which my scholarship had paid for. I left my Price blazer and my Panthers practice jersey hanging in the closet.

When it was all done, Bailey turned to me. "Look, Gil. Maybe they'll change their minds. Sometimes they do. Your dad should write that letter. The team really needs you. I really need you. Your the best roommate I've ever had here."

I nodded, but I still couldn't talk. I just stuck out my hand, and he shook it. "See you, Tom," I managed.

My dad smiled at me as we tossed the bags in the trunk, and he tried to make me believe things would turn out okay. This was all a misunderstanding, he said. It was true, but I must admit I didn't have much hope. He put his arm around my shoulders. Anyway, he said, it was Thanksgiving this week. I wouldn't miss that much school. I might be back on campus again before mid-term exams. Did I have my books with me, so I could keep up? Yes. Okay, then, we'll keep our fingers crossed.

As we headed down the long driveway, another car was coming in, a large black Ford. The face of the man behind the wheel was stern, even scowling, and I suddenly saw the resemblance to Rocky. It must have been his father, coming to get him.

Things could always be worse, I told myself.

Chapter Eight
Home for the Holidays

The best thing about the *Port Royal Lantern*, our newspaper at home, is that in wintertime, practically the whole sports section is devoted to ice hockey. They even run middle-school hockey news, so I was certain that the scores from the Thanksgiving tournament in Portsmouth would be in there; what's more, I could get them right away, since the *Lantern* had finally entered the twenty-first century and now had their own website, too. I wanted to see how my buddies back at Price were doing without Rocky and me. I sincerely hoped they would win, because I actually believed I might be back on the ice with them before Christmas. The team was nine and one, after all, with a great shot at the state championship in February. Anybody would want to be part of a team like that.

In the meantime, I tried to stay busy around Port Royal. On Thanksgiving day, my Uncle Gilbert (my mom's brother - I'm named after him) and Aunt Missy came over, and we watched parades and football on TV as my mother and father worked in the kitchen, crafting certain smells which made me realize some of what I had been missing out on at Price. We alternate ham and turkey each year, and this was a ham year, with ginger and cinnamon seasonings, sweet potatoes, snap beans my dad had picked from our garden in late summer, fresh-baked bread, blueberry pie (with berries my mom had put up in jars back in July) and pumpkin pie... a lot to be thankful for, come to think of it. But sometime in the middle of my second helping, I suddenly thought about the Panthers. Their first game in the Portsmouth Thanksgiving Tournament would take place that night. I felt a surge of excitement and disappointment at the same time, knowing I couldn't be with them. And I wondered if Rocky was somewhere feeling the same way I was just then.

It had snowed a couple of inches on Wednesday night, but my dad had cleared the driveway, and so after the dishes were done, my little sister Rose and I went out and played basketball. She's got a good shot, too; these days I can just barely beat her, even when I'm playing my hardest. Then we came inside again, winded and red-faced from the 30-degree air, and flopped down beside the fire in the den, where my dad was playing his jazz records for Uncle Gilbert. He does it every Thanksgiving, and Uncle Gilbert is such a nice man he pretends year after year that he has never heard those records before. Just like old times, I thought, as I lay there listening to the sweet clarinets and saxophones and trombones and the shushing of the cymbal.

After a little while, my dad said, "Well, Gil, it's Friday tomorrow. You know what that means."

"Yes," I said. "We can read in the *Lantern* about the Panthers. That tournament in Portsmouth."

"What? Oh, I guess you're right. But I was thinking instead about our little tradition. Remember?"

"Oh, right! The Christmas tree."

"I was up on Jacob's Hill the other day. Some good trees this year. Just prime for cutting. We'll get an early start."

It was one of those days I guess I'll always remember. It was still dark when we left the house. How many mornings have I left that house - usually to play hockey - when it was still dark outside? And the day... it always goes so quickly, especially in winter. But that morning seemed to last a good, long time. Speaking only a word now and again when necessary, we went into the garage and took our cross-country skis down from the rafters, wiping away the cobwebs with our gloved hands. Then we stepped into them, click-click, and taking up our poles, we were out in the dark, snowy field behind our house, striding along in utter silence.

It was a winding trail that led up the hill, and my legs were aching halfway up. I concentrated on my dad's back, with the axe in its leather cover snapped to his belt and a canteen of water slung over his shoulders. The higher we got, the thicker and fluffier and lovelier the snow became, and in the dawning light, it glistened like the snow in those little glass Christmas globes you shake up. When we reached the stand of fir trees above the town, the sun was even with us, and it threw a pink wash over everything - the stone houses below, the trees heavy with boughs of snow, and over my dad's face when he finally stopped and turned back to look at me.

"This is it," he said. "Sing out if you see a good tree."

It wasn't long before I had found two, side by side. Both were really nicely shaped and about the right size for our living room. One was a bit bigger, though, and my dad said it would be good to let that one grow another year. I agreed, but I took out my Buck knife, which I had on my belt, and while my dad went to work on the other one with the axe, I carved some words into the trunk of the larger tree: "Gil Gibbs, Price School Panthers..."

And suddenly, as the sun shone over the hill, I knew that we would never cut that tree, just as I knew that I would never again play for the Panthers. In the middle of his chopping, my dad looked over. He simply nodded and smiled, then resumed his work. When he was done and the tree was on its side, we drank some of the cold water from the canteen and prepared for the trip back.

Going downhill was easier, of course, but dragging the tree always created its own set of problems. It was my job to hold the back end, or the top, and guide it so as not to catch on any underbrush. It was hard: sometimes the tree had a mind of its own, and once both my dad and I fell down when it got snagged on a stump. We made it, though, and left the tree in the backyard to be cut and shaped later that morning. We would begin decorating later, too. Now it was time for breakfast.

The smells of coffee and coffee cake filled the house until it seemed the very walls breathed these aromas. Coming inside after the tree-cutting expedition was like stepping into the bath that you have longed for after many days out on a camping trip. My mother had brought in the newspapers, the *Bangor Daily News* and the *Port Royal Lantern*, and I remembered the hockey tournament again. I went straight for the *Lantern*, flinging back the pages, one... two... three... there it was. Middle School Scores. I moved my index finger down the page, and found it: "Portsmouth Middle School Tournament..." The Panthers had won in the first round, all right, 5-2, but what caught my eye next was the name that jumped out at me from the small print. According to the box score, Rocky Lufrano had scored a hat trick.

Must be a mistake, I thought. They somehow got the wrong name off the roster. Or else Coach Nelson had maybe given somebody else Rocky's number and had forgotten to change the roster. There had to be some explanation.

I couldn't eat. Later that morning, around eight, I asked my mom if I could put in a call to the phone in the lounge back at my dormitory at Price. There was a good chance someone would answer and could get Tom Bailey to the telephone to explain things to me. My mom took one look at the expression on my face and agreed to let me place the call.

It rang once, twice, three times... seven times in all before someone picked up. "Hullo?"

"Good morning, is Tom Bailey in his room?"

"Hold on. I'll check."

It was probably only three or four minutes that I waited, but it seemed like forever. Finally I heard Bailey's sleepy voice.

"Yeah?"

"Bailey? It's me, Gil."

"Gil? No kidding, is that really you?"

"It's me. How is everything there?"

"Everything's fine. You know, just trying to sleep in a bit. Had a game last night. A lot of the parents are here, since we weren't allowed a holiday. How was your Thanksgiving?"

"Oh, fine, everything's fine. Listen, Tom, I've just got to ask you something. I was looking at the newspaper this morning, and I saw the box score from the Price game. It says that Rocky Lufrano scored a hat trick."

"That's true, Gil. He did."

"What about the expulsion?"

"I don't know what to tell you, Gil. He's still playing. You left, and somehow he didn't. A lot of the guys are saying

83

that his dad got here last Sunday and pulled some strings. What with his older brother probably going to the NHL and all. Nobody knows for sure."

"Well... I guess it's great that you guys still have Rocky."

"A lot of the guys are upset about it, Gil. We want you to come back, too. Have you heard anything from the dean?"

"No."

"Well, maybe you will." But I could tell that things had changed already. There was a certain distant quality in Bailey's voice, and it wasn't just the miles between us. Maybe he already had a new roomie. We said our good-byes. He promised to write.

There were no jokes told.

As I hung up, my father came into the kitchen. "Hey, buddy. *Lantern* get here?"

"It's there on the table," I said. Then I went to my room, closed the door, and lay down on the bed.

I really couldn't figure it out. In everything I had ever tried, things had been fair. Sometimes, I knew I just wasn't good enough, like in the Port Royal school spelling bee. But at least I always had had a fair chance. I know that I am a fairly good hockey player. I may never make it to the NHL, or even make a college roster, but I've never been on a team when I didn't have something to contribute. I knew I had something to give to the Panthers, and I couldn't see why nobody wanted to give me a chance, nobody even wanted to hear what I had to say about things, the expulsion and all. Rocky was the one who had cheated, not me.

I think I was in my room most of that day. Sometime that morning, I heard my father's footsteps in the hall. They paused outside my door, and he lingered there. I could hear it when he put his hand softly on the knob, and I could almost feel his brain working as he wondered whether he should come in. And then he had made up his mind, and I heard his footsteps fading away again up the hall.

Chapter Nine
A New Team, New Life

I was dreaming about hockey again. I was skating down the ice, making moves which I could barely believe myself, going around one faceless defender, then another, then another, and finally streaking for the net as the buzzer sounded. I never got to take the shot, though. It was my alarm that was going off.

I looked over, expecting to see Tom Bailey across the room, adjusting his Price School red and blue necktie and frowning at me because I was already late. But it was my own room in Port Royal, with my books, my pictures, my shelves with hockey and baseball trophies glinting in the light that had seeped in meekly through the blinds.

It was Monday morning, and I had to go and register at the Port Royal Middle School, the local public school. It was not a bad place at all, of course, and I would know most of the kids there, if not all of them. Somehow I hoped that nobody would notice that I was just now showing up, and that nobody would ask me any questions. That wasn't likely, though – people are naturally curious. Then I thought maybe I could make up a story, tell the kids that I had been very sick these last few weeks, or that my parents had missed me so much they had insisted on me coming home, or even that they had abruptly decided they could not afford private-school tuitions. But it was useless - they all knew I had gotten a scholarship to Price.

Yet to me, the truth sounded pretty impossible, too: "Well, you see, I was falsely accused of cheating on a history test and got expelled. Kicked off one of the finest middle-school hockey teams in New England, even though I didn't do anything wrong." It was going to be a tough day.

I was greeted with silence in my first-period class, which was math. But by the mid-morning recess, the questions were coming like a snowstorm. Three of my old friends and hockey teammates, Hal Yates, Freddie Dixon, and Chipper Givhan, hovered around me at the bench by the outdoor basketball court, which was now slick with ice. I sat stone-faced, watching all the kids slide around or chase each other through the snow, as they interrogated me.

Freddie: "Geez, Gil, what happened? I heard you were kicking butt at Price."

"Same here," Hal said. "What are you doin' back here in Port Royal? We thought you'd made the big time and the next time we'd see you would be on TV."

"Everybody says Price will win the middle-school state championship this year," Chipper added.

I looked at their faces, and found that I couldn't lie to them. After only a moment's hesitation, I said, "I made a stupid mistake, you guys. I ended up someplace I shouldn't have with a guy who I thought was my friend. It's kind of a long story. What it all means is that they thought I was trying to cheat on a test. I was expelled."

Then something unspoken passed between them and me, like they understood me and yet knew I didn't want to talk anymore about it. And really, that was that; they didn't push it. Hal Yates just said, "Well, that's a shame, but you ought to come out for the Port Royal team. We could use you at forward. We've only won two games so far this season."

"Yeah," Chip said. "You're not gonna give up ice hockey are you, Gil?"

I looked across the courts and the playing fields, in their white winter robes with patches of yellow stems and brown mud showing through here and there, where the early snow had melted back a bit. "I hadn't thought about it. I hadn't thought that far ahead. It's all been so sudden." The bell rang, and we moved back toward the classroom buildings. Of course I didn't intend to give up hockey. For me, that would have been like giving up eating. I wondered if they were right, that it wasn't too late to go out for the Port Royal team, the Rangers. It might be nice, after all the pressure of playing for Price, to be on a public school team with no fancy facilities and no lofty expectations, and no coats and ties. That's the only bad thing about playing for a winner - everybody expects so much. It would sure be different: Port Royal practiced at an outdoor rink and used the youth league facility for all games, and there would be no huge cheering crowds with alumni and scouts, no nice embroidered red-and-gold jersey with a stitched emblem (Port Royal's colors were black and blue, with just the letters "P.R.M.S." stamped on the fronts of the shirts; there were no names on the backs). Maybe it would be a step back for me, in a way, but I began to believe it was one that I could live with... if I was still allowed to play.

I didn't have to wonder about it for long. In my last-period class, English, I received a note from the coach of the hockey team, Coach Ramsey. He was an old friend of my father's, and they had been teammates at the local high school. I still don't know how he found out I was back in town, but the note read,

Gil - I heard you are attending Port Royal Middle School these days. That's Price's loss, no doubt. Anyway, the deadline for accepting new players on public school teams is Dec. 3 - tomorrow. Talk to your dad about it tonight, and if you'd like to join the team here, I'm sure the Rangers could use you. - Coach Ramsey

But I felt that there was nothing to discuss. After all, when you receive a personal invitation from the coach, you're sort of obligated. Still, I told my father about it that night over dinner.

"Really?" he asked, taking a spoonful of carrots. "Coach Ramsey himself asked you to come out for the

team?" He glanced over and for some reason winked at my mom. "Well, I don't know, son. I thought this might be a good time for you to concentrate on your studies. Take a little time off from hockey and maybe re-apply to Price next semester."

Re-apply? I hadn't thought of it. In my mind I saw the stucco buildings, the rolling grounds, the hockey rink shining like a jewel, and the closet with the navy-blue jacket hanging in it. It made a nice memory.

"I don't think I could ever go back to Price now," I said. "And as far as my studies, I always do better when I'm playing hockey. You know that, Dad."

"Sure you want to play for little ol' Port Royal? After your experience with the Panthers, it might seem like going back to the minor leagues."

"Well... most of my friends are playing on the Rangers. Sure, the uniforms aren't nearly as nice, but... I just want to play. In fact, if I don't get to play hockey, I don't know what I'll do. I've been going crazy these last few days."

Now Dad smiled at me. "Okay, Gil. If you feel that strongly about it, it's all right with me." Then to my mom: "What do you say, hon'? Should we let the boy play some hockey?"

She reached over and put her hand on my arm. "I think Gil should play. I always thought he belonged right here anyway. Price is a fine school, but if you keep at your studies and do as well as you can in the Port Royal schools, you can go just as far."

And that was the end of the discussion. My mother's words had sealed the decision, as usual. When I went to bed that night, I had a feeling in me that I wouldn't call happiness… but it was a kind of contentment. Things were finally settled once again. I got up and went over to the window. Instead of the neatly kept grounds and the classroom buildings and the row of evergreens, I saw my backyard, with the treehouse, and Jacob's Hill in the distance, with its white collar of snow glowing in the moonlight. It was all real; I really was back.

I was back home.

"Sprint! Come on, sprint!"

The whistle shrieked. The cold rushed through my cage and bit into my face. Outdoor hockey practice was something I would have to get used to again, but it was good to be skating. It had seemed like forever.

The sky was streaked with clouds, a kind of wet, grey lathering that threatened snow. The wind seemed to roll in right over the boards and rush around the rink, blowing the sounds - the shouts of the players, the solid "whock" of the puck, and the crunching of steel blades on ill-groomed ice - around and around and then away into the thin air. Coach Ramsey's practice was looser, less regimented than Coach Nelson's, with a lot of skating and game-situation stuff, and I liked it. The guys were loose; they didn't seem to care that they had only won two games.

I worked out at center. I quickly saw that playing so much defense at Price had made me into a better forward. I felt that I could somehow see more of what was happening on the ice, and that I knew what was going on both in front of me and behind. Coach had me at second-line center, and at first I was worried that I was taking somebody else's spot. I said as much to Hal Yates, the winger on my line, as we waited for our turn at two-on-twos.

He shook his head. "We don't even have three complete lines. The other forwards and I have just been trading off at center. We know that's your position. Don't sweat it." He spit on the ice to show he meant what he said.

"If you say so. It's great to be skating up again." I picked up a puck with my stick and flipped it on the blade like a pancake.

It was our turn for the drill. "Let's go," Hal said.

I sent the puck to him as he crossed the blue line, and the defender came out on his side. Hal went around him with a quick move, and got the puck back to me in the slot. It dribbled off my stick for a moment, and so I took it on around the net, stopped short, and came back out the same side. Hal had managed to get open in the slot, and I sent the puck streaking toward him for a one-timer. And bang, just like that, it was in the back of the net.

"That's hockey!" Coach Ramsey shouted. "You guys see that? That's hockey!" Hal and I high-fived with our big gloves and went back to get in line again. Things were looking up at last.

After practice, the coach gave me my jersey - number 16, since that was the only one left - and a schedule of our remaining games. Something there caught my eye, and I could barely believe what I was reading: we were scheduled for a Christmas Eve tournament at the Price School for Boys. Teams participating – Port Royal Middle School, Fraley Catholic, and the Price School.

"Anything wrong?" Coach Ramsey asked.

"Um... no, sir. Just wanted to say thanks a lot for giving me the opportunity to play some more hockey, Coach."

"Good to have you on the team, Gil."

That night at dinner, I told my parents about the tournament at Price.

"Well, well," my dad said. "That's an interesting turn of events."

"They'll kill us," I said. "I think I'm going to like playing for Port Royal, Dad, but the truth is we don't belong on the same ice with the Panthers."

He folded his hands. "You never can tell, Gil. No sense in being beaten before you even play them." He was right, I knew. I had already seen some truly strange things happen in hockey. We would see.

And maybe, just for myself, I had something else to prove.

Chapter Ten
Rangers on the Road

Before long I had fallen into the rhythm of life again in Port Royal. There was school, practice, dinner, sleeping, waking, church on Sunday... Old jazz songs emanated from the den, or there was the thudding of a basketball out in the driveway as Rose practiced her jump shot (after my dad and I had cleared off the ice, of course), and the days shortened steadily as winter drew in around us. And hockey seemed fun again. We were playing a couple of games each week, and by the time school let out for Christmas break, I had a six-game scoring streak going. Hal and Freddie and I were working well together, setting each other up, one of us going in behind the net and feeding the puck out to the others, and we had won four of those six games. It was a looser style than Price's methodical, play-oriented game, but I liked it that way. I still didn't entertain any thoughts that we might beat the Panthers on Christmas Eve. We would be lucky, really, if we even qualified for the district playoffs in February.

And on Saturday mornings, I would go and help my dad with his Peewee team, opening the door in the box, setting the lines, and so on. It was nice - my younger cousin, Pete, played on that team, and so it still seemed like family to me. And something else kind of strange: I felt I learned more from watching my father, now that I wasn't playing for his team... or maybe it was just that I saw him in a different way. He really is a pretty good coach, I guess.

My parents are very much involved in the church, too – Grace Presbyterian Church, to be exact. My mother sings in the choir, and my dad has been head of the building and renovations fund drive for several years in a row. Since I was ten or so, they've always let me make my own choice about going, and I usually do attend services with them on Sundays. Besides the reading and the singing and praying and all, it's just a place where I feel comfortable: I like the smell of the polished wooden pews and the tall, white ceiling, and I like Pastor Greg. He's a genuinely nice man with an easy smile, and I somehow happened to run into him quite a lot in the weeks after my expulsion from Price. He came to many of the Rangers' games, and he hung around sometimes at our youth group meetings, and it took me a while to realize that he was making himself available to me, in case I wanted to talk about things. I didn't, but I'm certainly glad now to know that he was there if I had.

Christmastime in Port Royal, now that I think of it, is probably just like it is in small towns everywhere. Everybody decorates their houses, of course, and we have a big tree downtown in the middle of the square, and when it is to be lit, the mayor rides up to the top of the tree in a cherry picker and places the star on top. The town council and the churches collect canned goods and other stuff for the poor, and my mother is also very active in all of that. And the kids in our neighborhood act like kids in all neighborhoods probably do - a little anxious, a little crazy... and it all gets so quiet on Christmas Eve, as if the snow on the roofs of the houses is some sort of muffler.

That is, unless you're playing hockey. And so, my Christmas Eve is different, most years. That year, the year of the tournament at Price, the team ate a late breakfast at Coach Ramsey's house, and then we loaded into the school's little blue van (the only bus used by the middle school) and got on the highway headed south. Most of our families were going, too, including mine, and they would all be taking their own cars and showing up at the arena a little later. It struck me that this was the first time since I had left Price that I had been on a long road trip, and my stomach suddenly tightened up. The guys were talkative, chattering excitedly about the game and about what they might get for Christmas, but I sat quietly, and nobody talked to me. Maybe they sensed that I wanted to be left alone for a while.

In any case, I tried not to think about what had happened at Price or about Rocky being allowed to remain a student there, but of course, that's all I could think about. I realized the extent to which I had put it out of my mind, keeping myself so busy that I'd never had time to dwell on it. But now as I sat here, traveling the familiar way with nothing else to do, it all came back to me. I remembered the sinking feeling when the lights in Mr. Birnham's classroom came on and the security guard touched me on the shoulder. I saw again the stern, disappointed faces of Mr. Withers and the student council as they passed judgment on me, and my own shock and disbelief that such a thing could happen, that such a mistake could ever be made. But now I knew that such things did happen. And I wondered for the first time if they actually happen for some reason.

It was in the middle of these thoughts that I saw something weird out the window of the bus. There was a deer alone in the woods, a big, young male with the beginnings of his winter rack of antlers; he wasn't moving, but just standing in the snow at the edge of the trees, very still. Deer don't hibernate, of course, but it's still unusual to see one wandering about once winter sets in. Maybe hunger had driven him out of his evergreen bower. He didn't look as if he wanted to cross the highway, though – he seemed content, as if the woods on the other side of the roadway were really of no interest to him at all, but he had just come to have a look anyway. And maybe I am crazy, but I swear that he looked right at me, that our eyes met, and we gazed at each other for a few seconds. His head turned as the bus passed by, and staring back at him, I saw that he finally put his nose down, sniffed at the snow, and then turned back to the wilderness behind him. Even if it didn't mean anything, it took my mind off of the Price School and all of the trouble I'd had there, and I thought about that deer the rest of the way. I wondered what his life was like, back there in those woods, where it was quiet, and where school and hockey are not important to any of the creatures that live there. Their families are important to them, I guess, and maybe the deer do

103

have their own games and such that they play to pass the time when they're not searching for food. But I bet they don't worry much about who wins and who loses.

"Hey, champ, we're here."

Hal Yates was nudging my shoulder, and it was true. The van was turning into the gates at Price. For some reason, seeing the grounds and the buildings again made me smile.

"Better wipe that grin off," Hal said. "You're one of us now, you know. No thinking about the good ol' days."

I nodded. I knew that even in the NHL, where a guy gets paid a lot of money just for his professional skills, there is a feeling for a team. It happens right away. When you move to another team and you play against your old mates, you want to beat them just as badly as you wanted to win when you were with them. For the first time, I experienced that feeling firsthand. First we would have to get past Fraley Catholic, though, as we had drawn them for the first round. I remembered them well from my second game as a Price School Panther: they were a big, bruising team from Manchester, and we would have our hands full with them. Price had a bye and would play the winner of our game for the championship later that evening.

The bus pulled right up to the rink, and we filed out and then milled around on the sidewalk.

Coach Ramsey sidled over to me and said, "Well, Gil, how does it feel to be back?"

"Sort of strange, I guess."

"It'll be all right. Once you're on the ice, the game will be the only thing on your mind." Now he turned to the other players. "Boys, since Gil is the only one who's been here before, why don't we let him lead the way to the visitors' locker room. We 'll follow him."

We put our bags and sticks over our shoulders and headed inside. We passed along the corridor with the tall trophy cases, and I recognized Benny Lufrano's picture, and remembered hurrying past it so many times, trying to get to practice on time. Now I walked slowly, and I listened to the other players behind me, whistling and muttering about how fancy the arena was. The visitors' dressing room was directly across from the Panthers', and as I approached the door, someone was coming toward us down the hall.

It was Rocky. Of all the people I might have run into, it had to be him. He was wearing his red and gold sweats, and he looked up at me. He hesitated for just a moment, as if he wanted to say something, but then he put his head down and moved on past us.

"Who's that bruiser, Gil?" someone asked.

"Rocky Lufrano."

"Benny Lufrano's brother?"

"That's the one."

"I hear he's really good. They say he's got it all – speed, strength, toughness."

I heard myself say, "Yep," but I was thinking, he doesn't have it all.

Now, having seen his sad face once again, I understood that there were some things which I had that Rocky Lufrano would never have. For one thing, I had friends.

"Let's go, boys," Coach Ramsey said. "Let's get ready. It's time to play some hockey."

Our game started on time, and from the very first face-off, which Chip Givhan won for us, I knew that we would beat Fraley and that we would play Price for the tournament championship that night.

It wasn't easy, though. Fraley was a good checking team, and even Hal Yates, who was our biggest and toughest player, got knocked down a couple of times. Also, they had a lot of fans there who made a lot of noise, and when I spotted my mom and dad and sister in the seats with the other folks from Port Royal, I understood a bit more about small-town life. Then, just like Coach Ramsey had said, all I thought about was the game. In the first period, I took a good pass from Freddie in the neutral zone and was able to break free, with a couple of red jerseys hanging at either elbow, but I managed to get a half-step on them. I wasn't able to pull my stick back as much as I like to on my wrist shot, but I caught it hard enough that the goalie couldn't react. It took flight over his left shoulder and stuck in the top corner of the net, under the rear bar. It was up and down the ice after that, back and forth, until Hal hit a screaming slap shot late in the second period that no one seemed to see. Same spot - glove side, top shelf.

I skated over to high-five Hal. "Wow," I said. "I only heard that one."

He grinned. "The Yates Express," he said.

With a 2-0 lead in the third, our coach had us shift into a defensive mode. "Conserve some energy when you can," he told us. "Looks like we're gonna play another game tonight."

And it ended that way, with Port Royal's black and blue jerseys scrambling after the puck and clearing it away from Fraley Catholic's bigger, slower players. When the buzzer sounded, I looked for my parents once again. They were looking back at me, and we waved at each other. Rose was bouncing in her seat and clapping for us.

It was Port Royal's best game since I had joined the team. But we would have to be even better in just three hours or so. As casual as I had tried to be about it, I realized that I wanted to beat the Panthers. I wanted it for reasons I still cannot fully explain; you see, I wasn't ever really mad about the expulsion or even about Rocky staying and me going. Maybe it had to do with proving I belonged on the same ice with those guys. Whatever the real reasons were, it was clear to me now: I wanted it more than anything in the world, more than any toy I had ever wished for for Christmas, and with a kind of hunger which gnaws away at the deepest part of you.

Nothing else mattered. I wanted to beat the Panthers.

Chapter Eleven
The Best Game They Ever Saw

Everyone remembers one Christmas. All Christmases are fine, generally speaking, unless you're unlucky in some way. I am lucky. I don't remember a Christmas when I didn't have what I wanted. Well, maybe I didn't get exactly what I wanted some years, but I'm sure I've had more than a lot of other kids. Anyway, my special Christmas, the one I think I'll always remember, has nothing to do with presents under the tree or any of that stuff. It has to do with the hockey game between the Port Royal Rangers and the Price School Panthers, on Christmas Eve, when I was 13 years old. I'm still only 13, but there's no doubt that it was the one I'll never forget.

The arena was packed. It seemed that most of the boarders had returned to Price to see the game, and as always, there were a lot of alumni and teachers and parents in the stands. It was already getting loud. I looked up and found my mom and dad and little sister once again. They were there, of course, in the same spot. I wondered how many of the Price fans recognized me, or even remembered me. Things can change awfully quickly, and people forget.

During warm-ups, Tom Bailey and Clark Hightower skated over to say hello to me. They were good guys.

"Hi, Gil," Bailey said. "We wondered if you'd be playing for Port Royal."

"Sure," I said. "Gotta play somewhere."

"We've missed you, kid," Clark said. "Everyone talks about what a good back-checker you are. And Rocky's goal production has fallen off a bit, without you to do the deflection play with him."

"I'm sure he's getting by," I said, glancing over to where Rocky was stretching by the boards. Coach Nelson was standing beside him, and he happened just then to look up at me. He smiled and waved.

"Still playing defense?" Bailey asked.

"Nah, they've switched me back to center. That's what I always played back home."

"Could be interesting tonight," Clark said. He was trying to be nice, but I could tell from his attitude he expected Price to trample us. "See you, Gil."

Bailey remained for a moment. "I got a new roommate, Gil," he said. "Some guy from Portsmouth. He's not as good a player as you. Not as good a roomie, either."

"Thanks, Crunch." I grinned. "Talk to you after the game, huh?"

The clock ran out on warm-up time, and we piled into our box. The guys were excited. They were shouting and banging their sticks, and were more fired-up than I'd ever seen them. Coach Ramsey managed to get them quiet. He said, "Boys, this will be our toughest opponent this season. If we can beat these guys, I think we've got a good shot in the playoffs. From what I've seen from you boys lately, you're capable of winning tonight. Let's just play our game, utilize our speed. Defensemen, again, dump the puck and let our forwards chase it down. And watch their number 10. He's a great player." But they all knew about number 10; that was Rocky's number.

"One more thing," Coach Ramsey said. "All of you know that Gil Gibbs played for Price in a few games this season. I thought it would be appropriate to ask him if he has anything to say before we take the ice... Gil?"

I had to talk over the noise, as the Panthers were taking the ice and the crowd had begun to roar. I looked at my teammates' faces. "I just think..." I said, "I just think we should try and win it for our families. And for everybody back home. Let's show them all."

Their shouts of approval were drowned by the crowd, but I could see it in their eyes. We were ready. I sat down to wait for my first shift.

On the face-off, Rocky stuck his shoulder into Chip Givhan and took control of the puck. He whipped it back to his defenseman and then made a burst for the blue line, receiving the puck again and skating alone into our zone. About 15 feet out, he took a hard wrister that Tim Washell gloved. The whistle blew, and the crowd let go its collective moan at this near-miss.

"Whoa," said Hal Yates, who was next to me in the box. "That was fast."

It was fast, all right. And it never let up. Rock had two more shots on his first shift, and the pace barely slackened when we changed lines. On an offsides face-off, I lined up against Bobby Horner, who was small but fast. He was the one whose navy blazer Bailey had once switched with mine, as a joke. But we weren't smiling now. I dug for the face-off and won it, scooting it back to Hal. In turn, he took it over to Freddie Dixon, who crossed the blue line with it and tried to cut back on the defenseman, who just managed to get a piece of the puck. Freddie made a desperate attempt to get the puck to me as I headed into the slot, but it was just out of my reach, and the Price goalie leapt catlike out of his crease and froze it. After that, the whole shift was up and down, up and down, the puck changing possession at least six times during the shift, and I was awfully winded when we finally went to the bench. We had only two lines, with two extra guys, so I knew that at some point I'd be matched up with Rocky. Better rest. I reached for my water bottle.

Price's third line was every bit as good as their second. Hal and Freddie were skating their hardest, and I could see that they, too, were getting weary. It had a lot to do with having played one tough game that day already; it was clear that the Price skaters were fresher, but they seemed so much quicker overall. I wondered if I had looked that fast when I played for them. It was all our players could do to just get a stick in and poke the puck away at the crucial moment.

It was the last shift of the first period when I was matched up with Rocky Lufrano. As we leaned in for a face-off down in the Panthers' zone, he did not look at me or speak to me, but I didn't expect him to. He never talked during a game, not even to his own teammates. You've always got to expect to be punished in a face-off with the Rock, and he stuck his shoulder into me and spun me around, and swiped the puck right out from under my feet. It dribbled toward Tom Bailey, who snapped it back to Rocky. I was with him every stride, bothering him, bumping him, but he knew how to keep his body between me and the puck, and he was able to make his pass back into the slot. Then he did something I had seen him do many times, so really I should have been ready for it. As soon as he got rid of the puck, he changed directions and checked me hard into the open ice. I went sprawling on my back, my helmet banging on the hard surface, as Rocky did a quick stop and used his blades to fling ice up into my face, just to finish me off. As I got to my feet, I couldn't hear the crowd, but I could see some guys sitting by the glass clapping and cheering wildly. I thought, "Geez, it was just a check... but then I realized that they weren't even looking at me. They were cheering because Tom Bailey had scored off of Rocky's assist.

I hadn't seen it, of course, but later our goalie, Tim Washell, told me it was a simple re-direction of the puck, a deflection play. I always wondered if he had learned to do it from me, but then I thought... no. Everything Rocky ever did on the ice when I saw him play was sheer gut instinct.

The important thing, though, was that now we were down a goal. There was just time for the face-off, which I managed to win this time, and our defenseman sent the puck in, and then the horn sounded to end the period.

As it often goes with a close game, the second period is more or less a blur to me now. I just remember chasing down the puck quite a lot, shoveling it off to the wing, skating up ice, then having to skate back again when the Panthers cleared. And I remember being more tired than I have ever been on the ice, feeling as if my legs would stop working at any moment, that I'd fall over in an exhausted heap and they'd have to carry me off. But we all kept going. Freddie Dixon took two strong slapshots in the period, I remember, and their goalie just barely gloved one, and the other hit the crossbar. When the horn sounded again and Price retained their one-point lead, the crowd was all one voice. It was that feeling like nothing else exists in the whole wide world except the place where you are, and nothing else is of any importance except what you are doing. It's strange now to think that just then, most people were sitting down to Christmas Eve dinner. And if you really want to go into it, maybe in other places in the world, people were already asleep, or else it was still daytime. But there was a terrific hockey game going on where we were, and I was in the thick of it.

It seemed that we had our second wind. On the bench, I asked Hal Yates, "You okay?" He nodded. Everyone still looked determined. I knew we had a chance.

I've heard just about every kind of speech there is for a hockey coach to give. But so far, Coach Ramsey's few words before the third period that night have been the most meaningful to me - even more so, I guess, than stuff my dad used to say when I was on his team. It was the situation that made it different, I guess. Anyway, Coach Ramsey said, "Guys, we've already done a lot better tonight than anyone expected us to do. No matter how it turns out, you should be proud of yourselves. And you should be proud because tonight you've shown everyone what real hockey is all about. It's not about a fancy rink and fancy uniforms and an expensive program. It's about people just like you in small towns just like yours, playing because they love to play. You're already winners, in my opinion. Now, let's finish out this game and go home to our families and have Christmas back home in Port Royal."

Hal Yates is one of those players who tries things sometimes you know he doesn't really possess the skills to do, yet he does them anyway out of sheer stubbornness. And that's what he showed on his first shift in the third, when he clipped a loose puck around Clark Hightower, who is fast on his skates, and went around him and drove toward the net. Hal didn't even try to deke, but lifted the puck like a rocket over the goalie's right shoulder; it hit the back of the net so hard the twine shot back, and the puck bounced back out into the crease, as the siren went off. And so a minute and a half into the last period, it was a 1-1 game.

More hard skating, on my first two shifts, up and down, with nothing to show but heavy breathing and burning legs, but I could feel that I was building up to that moment when I would feel no pain, when nothing would be of any importance except the puck and the net. I came to the bench again, sat down, and waited.

Rocky Lufrano was on the ice for most of the period. He had two ripping shots at our goal and two thundering checks in the neutral zone. Freddie Dixon was so shaken up he had to come to the box, and I went out at wing, in place of him. Things were happening now on the ice with such speed

that there were only the sounds - the sharp shushing of metal on ice, the rattling of the snaps on helmets and shoulder pads, the whock of the puck against a stick. And yet, to me, the game seemed to slow down, to be almost in slow motion. I was seeing everything then, and the light was very bright, yet the sounds of the game told me that everything was happening at great speed.

When I sat on the bench again, I looked around. I looked at the action taking place on the ice, and it all made sense in a weird way I'd never noticed. And for the only time since the game had started, I looked up in the seats for my mom and dad and sister. Everyone was standing up now, and finally I spotted them behind some guys who were waving a Price School banner. I've never asked him about it, but I could swear that my dad looked back at me and nodded.

A whistle sounded an offsides, and I went out for the last two and a half minutes with our power line. Before I leaned over to take the face-off, I looked to either side of me: Freddie and Hal were there, looking intently at the puck in the ref's hand. Rocky skated up opposite me, and for the first time that night, our eyes met. Even now, I'm not sure I could say what I saw. I saw a boy, a lot like me, I guess. But there was something else, an acknowledgment from him - he would go far in ice hockey, there was little doubt of that, and perhaps I would not, but on this particular night we had played even-up. None of the stuff about the expulsion counted anymore. Everything we had and believed was right here, in this next face-off.

He won it. His defenseman, number six (who must have been the player who had replaced me, come to think of it) accepted the puck and cradled it, considering his options carefully. And just as Freddie skated in to attack, the defenseman sent the puck back to Rocky, who was breaking toward the blue line. It was the same play they had used all night, a give and go, and I was ready for it. I took the puck neatly away, having to wait for Freddie to come back onside, and then I just dumped it into their corner. Hal Yates skated for all he was worth, but he couldn't beat the Price defender to the puck. And here came Rocky again, up along the boards. I managed to catch him with a sort of half-check, as he used his size to absorb it and then cut back again into the middle. But one of our players had gotten their first, and he sent it ahead into their defensive zone. They took advantage of Hal and Freddie having to scramble again back over the blue line, working the puck between them, with one, two, three crisp passes, the disk ending up on Rocky's stick as he came over the blue line. I held my breath as he loaded up his wrist shot.

But Tim Washell was lucky; the puck caromed off of the top of his helmet, over the net, and into the glass behind it. Instinctively, I did not break for the loose puck, but skated ahead into the neutral zone. I took a quick look up at the clock. We were under a minute now. I could see Chip Givhan, our defenseman, puffing as he struggled after the loose puck behind our own net. Then with a tremendous effort, with Rocky bearing down on him, he cleared the puck up to me.

I found myself alone, crossing the blue line. I heard the defenseman gasping behind me. I shot the puck from about ten feet out, and it ricocheted off of the knob of their goalie's stick. Number six, my replacement at Price, went into the corner after the puck. I was standing in the slot, all by myself, and their defenseman made a terrible mistake. Or maybe he had trouble digging the puck along the edge of the board, where the ice was not so good. Anyway, he did something I'll always remember, and for which I will always feel sorry about, really. He passed the puck right to me. The Panthers' goaltender never had a chance. I one-timed it, and hit the upper right-hand corner of the net. I stood there, looking at the puck as it made the twine shiver and then dropped to the ice inside the goal. Then the buzzer sounded.

We had won the game, 2-1.

When we lined up for the handshake at center ice, the crowd was filing silently out of the arena. But I could hear my little sister's voice as clear as a bell:

"Way to go, Gil!" she shouted.

As I skated past Tom and Clark, both of them congratulated me. "Great game," they said. "Great game."

Tom added, "Come up and visit us sometime, Gil." I nodded. But I knew I would never come back to the Price School.

Rocky was the last player I shook hands with. He had taken his helmet off. "Great game," he said. "You really are still a Panther, you know. I don't care what anyone else says." Then he smiled and skated away.

I had been just about to say, "Nope. I'm a Ranger now." But when I think about it, maybe I always will be a Panther in a way. I'll always have what I learned there. My dad came into the locker room to see me. He waded over, through the giddy players and the piles of equipment, and he patted my shoulder. He had only one thing to say:

"That was the best game I ever saw, son. Bar none."

I nodded in agreement.

"Let's go home," I said.

Chapter Twelve
The Ride Back

A light snow was coming down when our old Bel-Air turned out of the drive and headed up on the highway. In the back seat, Rose was staring at me, the way she does sometimes when she's especially proud of something I've done. Finally I said,

"Come on, Rose. It was just a game."

Then for some reason, all four of us, Mom and Dad included, burst out laughing at that. It was pretty ridiculous, I guess. I had played that game as if my life had depended on it.

"Just a game?" my dad said. "That's very interesting."

"Sort of like Christmas Eve being just another night," my mom added. I had almost forgotten about Christmas. As we drove along, we could see the lights on the houses in the little villages and vales.

Things had certainly changed for me since Thanksgiving. I guess it just goes to show that things often do work out okay. I was happy playing for the Rangers, and I realized that I had never really fit in at Price anyway. I liked the place, all right, and I knew it was a great school, but it wasn't really for me.

I suppose I should tell what happened over the rest of that season. After all, it is spring now, and it's all over, and I'm looking ahead to baseball season and then eighth grade at Port Royal Middle School. It's funny the way a season will end, and there are new things to do and think about. But that Christmas tournament at Price was something I'll never forget. As it turned out, we did make the district playoffs, but we were defeated in the opening round. We never played quite as well again as we had played against the Panthers. And speaking of the Panthers, they went on to win the New Hampshire state championship, with only two losses all season. Rocky was voted the Player of the Year at the middle-school level.

But to me, the best part of all was the ride back home on Christmas Eve, the night of the tournament. My heart was calm, and I was with the people I cared about most, and as the road disappeared behind us, I felt that part of my past was falling into place in my memory. And the countryside was swaddled in Christmas lights and in snow, and the scent of firewood seeped through the vents of the Bel-Air, and my dad tapped the steering wheel to the tune of some big-band CD he had popped in. I had nothing in the world to worry about now.

And as we came around the last curve, the streets of Port Royal were empty, though the red and green and white lights glowed against the drifting snow. The whole town was asleep, waiting for Christmas morning to come.

Jeff Trippe is a freelance writer, illustrator, and a part-time musician; he also teaches literature and writing. His previous books include *This Brittle Existence* and *Lawsuits of the Rich and Famous*. He lives with his wife and daughter in Yarmouth, Maine.

www.ingramcontent.com/pod-product-compliance
Lightning Source LLC
Chambersburg PA
CBHW060942040426
42445CB00011B/971